THE
LONE WOMAN
AND
OTHERS

THE LONE WOMAN AND OTHERS

Constance Urdang

UNIVERSITY OF PITTSBURGH PRESS

Published by the University of Pittsburgh Press, Pittsburgh, Pa. 15260
Copyright © 1980, Constance Urdang
All rights reserved
Feffer and Simons, Inc., London
Manufactured in the United States of America

Library of Congress Cataloging in Publication Data

Urdang, Constance.
    The lone woman and others.

    (Pitt poetry series)
    I. Title.
PS3571.R3L6   811'.54   80-5261
ISBN 0-8229-3430-2
ISBN 0-8229-5320-X (pbk.)

Some of these poems have appeared in the following periodicals: *American Poetry Review, Ascent, Focus/Midwest, Gallimaufry, The Hampden-Sydney Poetry Review, The Missouri Review, New Letters, The New Republic, Open Places, Poetry Miscellany,* and *Poetry Now.*

"Driving to Mexico" originally appeared in *The Nation.* "The Day the Houses Sank" originally appeared in *Poetry* (June 1971). "The Old Maid Factory" was originally published in *Poetry Northwest,* vol. XVI, no. 2 (Summer 1975). "His Sleep" was copyrighted by Washington and Lee University, reprinted from *Shenandoah:* The Washington and Lee University Review with the permission of the Editor.

"Little Requiem for a Witch" is reprinted from *The Carleton Miscellany,* copyrighted by Carleton College, October 8, 1965. "Leaving Mexico One More Time" is reprinted by permission from *National Forum,* vol. LIX, no. 2 (Spring 1979), p. 35. "Feme Sole," "Pity," and "The Invention of Zero" are reprinted by permission from *New England Review,* vol. I, no. 4 (Summer 1979).

*The publication of this book is supported by grants
from the National Endowment for the Arts
in Washington, D.C., a Federal agency,
and the Pennsylvania Council on the Arts.*

For my brother

CONTENTS

CONTENTS

CONTENTS

ONE

THE LONE WOMAN
OF SAN NICOLAS ISLAND

1

Somewhere inside me lives
the lone woman of San Nicolas Island
"good looking
and about middle-age," speaking
no known language
but continually
sending forth a soft babble
like a stream over stones

During the uncounted years
after her abandonment
she survives
makes the days pass, lives
on shellfish and seal-fat, dresses
in skins and feathers of wild ducks

From time to time
she glimpses a ship on the horizon
when it steams out of sight
she throws herself on the ground, weeping

2

What remains to her
of the lost child
whose cries she heard, or imagined,

The babe hungry and not fed,
without understanding, exposed, motherless,
wailing, and not comforted?

Not a hair of its head
not a handful of bones
not a stone

3

3

With desperate strength,
tearing herself
from the arms of her rescuers
she plunges back into the wilderness of herself
as if it were a burning house
but finds nothing to save

Only the little waves lapping at the beach
only the leaves whispering in the sun
and the cold stars at nightfall
and the wind crying in the reeds

4

If, like the wild dogs
she is cast out
forsaken
like the serpent, cursed,
an amputated limb
lopped from the body of mankind

Then exile, anchorite,
solitary as a nun
estranged, unvisited,
no longer daughter, sister, mother,
she knows no one,
her voices are her own

5

In a dress of feathers,
the plumage of the green cormorant,
iridescent, lustrous as satin,
she is Queen

She has made
an ornament of stone
to wear between her breasts

On the walls of a shallow cave,
she records her country's history
ships sighted, storms, triumphs of the hunt,
one inexplicable eclipse of the sun

Though the scratches in the rock
are without meaning
to the wild dogs, her subjects,
courtiers, and only companions,
she survives, leaving
in the wilderness
"the print of a slender human foot"

6

If once a boatload beached on her shore
would she hide herself?
Would she, afterward, grieve
because they will not come back, or
fearlessly bestride her kingdom
which is within me?

PORTRAIT

Trespasser in my own house,
my own alter-ego,
I'll never catch myself.

I'd steal my own treasures:
the silver ring set with a carnelian,
the little book bound in tooled leather.

I arrange myself like an odalisque
on the model's throne
and dare them to paint me.

Some days I impersonate myself
and walk in the city
collecting wolf-whistles and propositions.

I look for myself in the supermarket
among the stout mammas
in the odor of oranges and bananas.

In a crazy-quilt of weeds
I invade my own back yard.
Not even the dog knows me.

FEME SOLE

What is she doing in the body of this other,
Under a dusty wig,
Struggling to find happiness
In the fifty-six classical positions?

Traveler in the landscape of her own body,
She is nowhere at home.
When the long evenings come down,
Implacable, in hotel rooms, where she waits,

She thinks she will emigrate to a tropical country,
Or dedicate her life to the poor,
Or marry the delivery boy
Who comes with an armload of flowers, but not for her.

Under a costive sky
In the kitchen of the deserted apartment
A faucet is dripping.
This woman is dangerous.

BEING A WOMAN

I have resented the woman in the
woman, having to be her, sitting
in the bathtub surrounded by
herself, resented
breasts, hips, buttocks,
resented flesh itself, womanflesh,
wanting to go incognito
without ornaments or emoluments
abstract as a grassblade
as a piece of straw

BIRTH

Before, there was one
Without a name

I killed it
It had no heart

One wrenched away
With a single cry

My body floated
Inches above the bed

Another drowned
In freshets of blood

It was warm in the bed
But a cold hand touched my heart

In the eyes of the newborn
I see an ancient woman

She thinks nothing was
Before she came.

HIS SLEEP

His legs are positioned for flight
Knees bent like a runner's
One higher than the other
Muscles relaxed now, slack
On the long bones, femur and tibia

Elbows bend to the shape of his dream
One arm embraces the pillow
The other grasps at nothing, until
His fist strikes the mattress
Setting off a bed of earthquakes

His night-breathing is louder than speech
It rattles in his throat
Like the ghost of croup-kettles,
Heaving him over, exposing the vulnerable parts,
Tufted ribs, soft belly, idle sex

Born new and naked every morning
Soon he'll wake with a groan
Every limb flying out in startled protest
And squint wryly into the light
Of our common life

DAUGHTERS

If I were the mother of twenty-two beautiful daughters
My crimson heart,
Pasted on twenty-two lace-paper valentines,
Would threaten to tear apart those delicate cages
Decorated with blossoms and impossible flying babies,
And stain them with real blood, pulsing, arterial.

Awakened every day by twenty-two beautiful daughters,
I should rise in a froth of song from my pillow
Like Venus rising out of the sea
In a garland of nymphs and naiads!

All day, their beauty illuminated
Like the eleven hundred virgins of St. Ursula
On a page of some rare old missal,
My daughters would drowse
In the inexhaustible hum of their own voices

Until, seeing them swooping and skittering,
Twittering, en route to their dreams,
My pincushion heart, obstinate, swollen heart,
Heart heavy as the rock of Sisyphus,
Would tear apart into twenty-two pieces,
If I were the mother of twenty-two beautiful daughters.

THE RUNAWAY GIRLS

Somewhere out in the country
Is the hiding-place of the runaway girls:
The angry, impertinent daughter, the sullen pupil,
The sister left out of the brother's marriage,
The one beaten black and blue by a drunken father,
The one who was caught making out on the living room sofa,
The one in the family way, the one with no family,
Defiant tomboy and recalcitrant nymph,
The hungry, the reckless, the bored, the desperate,
All find their way to that place

None of the fathers knows where to find them;
Waiting back home, the mothers
Are sleepless in waterfalls of their own hair
And watched by kitchen windows reflecting images
Of the long roads leading to unimaginable cities,
And out of the cities, the highways reaching out
Into distances where the runaway girls
Become so small they cannot be distinguished,
And their tiny voices fade across the landscape
And a thin wind stirs in the sad curtain

For daughter won't come home to her dear daddy
And sister has disappeared, all the little sisters
Have gone away for good and won't come back.
In the hiding-place of the runaway girls
Under a pale green moon
Languid as leaves, they dance their innocent games,
Browse among dreaming grasses
Spellbound before looking-glasses
That, timeless, silent, incorporeal,
Give nothing back but their own soft, enamored faces.

CHANGE OF LIFE

Ashes of roses, forsythia bones,
tulips with blackened teeth,
let me read in you
what has become of the young girl in the legend
who so craved honey
that her entire life was changed by it

When she lay down
roses sprang from her side
her body became a trellis
for ardent tropical blooms
with corollas so deep
you could drown in them
disappearing in those mysterious caves

In this way the bees found her;
in the laboratory of the hive
they are transforming her into an old woman
drained, shriveled, and unsexed
like a quince-blossom mutilated by the frost.
She has been rendered to her essences
her voice comes to you through the lips of a crone

ON LOOKING INTO
CULPEPER'S HERBAL REMEDIES

Praise herbs that make barren women fruitful,
That make the heart merry and drive away melancholy,
That break the stone in the kidneys and drive it forth,
That mollify inflammations;
Herbs that comfort those that are troubled with swooning,
And are profitable to those with an old cough,
That temper the heat of the liver
And warm cold griefs.

Praise herbs that, taken in a broth, keep lean and lank
Those apt to grow fat; and heal
Those outwardly bruised, or inwardly,
By falls or blows; praise such infusions
As are dropped into the eye for preserving sight
Or used to bathe the feet of travelers
And those whose long running causes weariness;
Herbs that defend the heart.

In wineglassful doses, or ointments, or poultices,
Praise the *materia medica*, "so well known
That it needs no description," balm
Of the weedy wayside, the poor man's dispensary.

LITTLE REQUIEM FOR A WITCH

I knew a witch who used to stroll
Next to the beach
In the mild sweet summer evenings
With the husband she had carved out of wood;
His painted pale blue eye was fixed
On the pale blue saucer-rim
Where the water became sky;
The witch, the wife
Twittered and glittered like a wind-harp.

Together, they went past
Pebbles, snail-shells, mussel-shells, crab-shells,
Driftwood, beach-grass, brilliants of broken glass
Tangled in the seaweed alongside the water,
Mother-of-pearl, till it swallowed the sun.

Now they are gone.
No sand takes the print of their feet.
Her high, harsh cries, like a seagull's, are not heard
On any of the uncounted shores of the world;
Not even her ghost walks abroad in henna and rouge.
The painted light is gone out of the husband's eye.
Where the round red sun slides nightly under the water,
I want them to be remembered, I want to remember.

THE PAPER FLOWERS

She is waiting
for the doorbell to ring
(if she can hear it),

Conjuring up
grandchildren with papier-mâché smiles
and loud, blurred voices;

In the unsparing sunset light
she grows uneasy.
Already memory like a fine white powder

Has settled on the polished wood;
the fabric of the sofa is disintegrating,
spilling out Grandma's white hair;

The clock has a face like a clown,
its hands threatening
with meaningless gestures.

In the silence, only
the rushing of water, which has
"an astonishingly long memory."

Soon all that will remain
will be these paper flowers,
so pale,

Even their leaves bleached out,
with veins like threads
and a faint flush at the heart.

THE INVISIBLE WOMAN

Now that I have become invisible
I can go anywhere
Flow through crowds and cracks
Slide past gateposts
Insinuate myself through
Chinks in the wall
Pry into corners
Look boldly into windows
To watch how other people live
Eavesdrop in full view
Nothing can keep me out
No one knows what I do

I walk through the square
Stare as long as I please
At lovers on park benches
Or, on the beaches,
At beautiful brawny boys
No one knows what I see
No one sees what I do
Nothing is taboo
Except that even if I wanted to
I cannot reappear
Can't repossess
The flesh I willingly gave up for this

THE OLD WOMAN

Sits turned away from the window;
She is looking at the wall
Without seeing it.
She thinks her son is coming
With a bouquet of roses,
With orchids, and a box of candy,
Bringing his heart, still pulsing, hot,
In a crimson gift box.

Soon the old woman
Will think it is dinner-time.
Her nostrils will fill
With the nourishing smell of chicken soup,
Homemade noodles, and a little wine.
Satisfied, having eaten nothing,
She will think it is night.
Everything darkens.

She will uncover herself
And arrange the body on the bed,
If she can remember how to do it.
Already under her breastbone
A fist is opening and closing.
She thinks it will choke her.
She thinks no one will come.
It is choking her.

PITY

She wouldn't want pity.
What good is it to her?
She'd rather have a pair of gloves
To smooth on over her rings.

If you gave her pity
She'd exchange it next Saturday
For a peach-colored lacy nightgown
Or half-a-dozen monogrammed handkerchiefs.

She wouldn't even give it away
To the cripple on the corner
Who strikes sparks from the sidewalk
With an iron leg-brace.

If hers were the last house on the last street
She wouldn't give it house-room.
Pity can take care of itself, she'd say,
I'll do the same.

THE BOSS-VIRGIN

The boss-virgin has decided to make a man
Out of hides and beads
His whiskers will be grouse feathers
His heart will be a pebble
She will stuff him with sand

He will walk on stilts
He will carry a searchlight in his head
Having no need to eat he will be toothless
His eyes will be quartz crystals
Reflecting light without seeing it

No other woman will want him
Without genitals he will father nothing
Inside his skull the sand shifts a little
When she dandles him on her knee
And her voice speaks from his belly

THE OLD MAID FACTORY

This is the factory
Where they manufacture old maids
At one end of the assembly line
The women are jostled into their places
They wonder where they are going
What will happen to them
One says, "Where is my sister?"
But the foreman is not permitted to answer

First she will be hollowed out
Her juices extracted
Her natural organs replaced
By parts she is not permitted to name
Her five senses
Are replaced by substitutes
Guaranteed non-inflammable
Non-toxic
Her sister is replaced by a substitute

At the end of the assembly line
The old maid minces out
Into what she calls America
She has forgotten she is a woman
She has no sister
In her shriveled brain
Something murmurs that life is an accident
She wonders how it happened to her

FIVE-FINGER EXERCISE
ON AN OLD PIANO

The woman at the piano broods
In the emptiness of the house at six o'clock,
Hour when thin, atmospheric ghosts
Trailing gauzy shawls, whisper
Beyond half-closed doors, restless,
Just out of earshot, inarticulate;
Hour of echoes, of missing persons,
Hour of being far from home,
Hour when the night comes down
And shadows lengthen, pointing away,
And darkness reaches up out of the earth;

Once she was like you,
A girl strumming the ballad of difficult loves.
Her instrument cradled between innocent knees,
She was a nymph in the suburban garden;
A young woman, heavy with future life,
Its weight holding her to the earth.
Now she fingers an exercise of interiors,
Chords of patterned carpets, études of furniture,
Daylight filtering a fitful illumination
Through curtained windows, and the glass gives back
A face domesticated, half-familiar,
Dimly glimpsed in the shadows of six o'clock.

ALONE

for Catalina de Erazu (b. 1685), who escaped marriage and the convent
to drive mules on the highways of the New World

In her own first person
Singular, anonymous, sister
To all or to none,
She renounces womanliness,
All softness, delicacy, all warmth;
Her road is harsh and solitary, she stumbles;
The end is not in sight.

Why should she pray
To the patroness of widows,
Spinsters, and solitary women?
She is not bereaved.
She will not take their bait.
Obstinate as her mules,
She insists on her own being.

She has sloughed off
The metaphors of girlhood,
Rejected the bridegroom,
Refused the wedding-veil.
She resists the garden's sweet decorum,
The marriage of the gladiolus and the lily,
Images shimmering on a still pond.

She plans an elopement
With no lover or husband;
Creeping in secret from her maiden room,
A ladder under the window,
She will escape with herself.
She will march to the drumbeat
Of a single stubborn heart.

They will try to seduce her
With cooking smells, with the tug of tiny fingers;
Threaten her with barrenness,
Accuse her of secret vices,
Sniggering, call her deserted, shame her,
Name her a witch, drown or burn her,
Or try to force, and take her;

In the company of men
Her secret, her sex, is safe
Only while they do not suspect.
Striding along the dim road
She thinks she can walk forever.
She asks no special privilege.
She will elude them all.

Footloose among outcasts,
She will sleep under frosty stars.
Warmed by the indifferent bodies of animals,
Lulled by their breathy sighs
And her own dying fires,
She will laugh, curse, scratch herself,
And find the living flesh under her shirt.

TWO

SOMEBODY'S LIFE

Somebody's life going by
Like the landscape seen through a train window,
Houses, a level crossing, a school,
Clustered store-fronts, gas pumps like twin sentinels,
A clump of dusty trees, and the pale fields ready for winter
Glimpsed through the old glass pane
Of an old daycoach, gritty with soot
And the stale reek of monotonous journeys.

Somebody's life is spelled out
Along the ragged coastline
Past salty blue estuaries;
Here a woman, bundled up against the wind
In a man's torn sweater,
Is harvesting stiffened clothes from a clothesline.
By the time she pitches them into her basket
With reddened hands
The train will have passed.

The windows of tenements are crowded with somebody's life.
A single red geranium blooms on the sill;
In the darkness behind it, voices
Carry on the same old argument.
Later, someone will remember
The rumble and clatter of the lighted train
Already slowing down for a stop at the terminal,
That used to punctuate his nights.

FAMILY LIFE: 1

Grandmother is crying
With a sound like the mewing of seagulls
She thinks her cheeks will turn to dough
Gray with too much handling
Through which her tears have scored deep channels

She is searching hopelessly
Through the pockets of her flesh, distended
With hard use, where lie concealed
Among a litter of tissues and strings
Heal-alls for she has forgotten what complaints

When her old chin trembles
A faint fluttering of compassion
Tugs hurriedly inside me
In the amniotic fluid of her grief
Something is fighting for life

I must escape her tears
They want to engulf me like the tentacles
Of some vast boneless creature
That swims languid and lethal
Through deep canyons on the ocean floor

FAMILY LIFE: 2

Her old man sits in the window
She thinks he is deaf
Because he does not look up at her step
She screams a single obscenity in his ear
He does not look up
Through a megaphone
She screams two obscenities
He scratches his nose
She comes toward him
With a dish of hot noodles
And empties it on his head

Tendrils of steaming noodles
Wreathe his brow
He sighs gently and lifts tender blue eyes
To her face suffused with rage
He is wondering what is making her so angry
Seeing his pale eyes turned toward heaven
She thinks now he is blind
So she smashes the dish into thirty-six pieces
On top of his unresisting skull

Now she thinks he is dead
She accuses herself
"Help! Murder!" she screams
There is blood on the noodles
He hasn't noticed
He sits in the window reading the paper

FAMILY LIFE: 3

The child believes mother is a tree
From which he picks
Out-of-season fruits
New shoes
Tickets to the baseball game
When nothing comes
He shakes her roughly
She does not tremble
He thinks her gnarled old roots
Are too deep and strong
He kicks her and tells her how ugly she is
Still nothing happens
She does not fall down
He wishes she would topple suddenly
He'd chop off her branches
He'd slash her bark with his knife
Her roots would clench foolishly
In the empty air
And he'd have everything he ever wanted

She says his numbers mean "lazy,"
"Bad father," and "poor";
Besides, his palms are sweaty
And he will soon be bald.
Did he ever say he loved her?

She makes him sit in the corner
With his face to the wall,
But when her friends come, she says,
He walks out in a torn undershirt.

Another person's father
Might have the numbers
For "money," "ice cream," and "good luck."
He tries to remember
What he is doing here.
She kicks his shins to make him look at her
And screams in his ear she will
Marry the garbage-man.

THE MIRACLE-FACTORY

Papa's got a job in a miracle-factory
downtown someplace, one of those streets
west of the avenue, in an old
building taller than God. There's a marble lobby, two
elevators behind brass gates, a newsstand,
and a draft whenever anyone pushes through
the glass revolving doors. Upstairs
after the corridor, damp, windy, cold
RING BELL COME IN the loft
looks at an airshaft. Soot settles softly, like snow.

I went there once with Papa. Standing soldierly
put out my hand to the boss, said, How d'you do.
I didn't like it much. The boss said, Boy,
when you grow up I want you to remember
making miracles is just like any other line, profit and loss,
also supply and demand. You got to sell
the product, make them believe
in it! He shook my hand.
Papa said later, He's the boss, without
the boss, no factory. Remember that.

DUSK TO DAWN

Mrs. Wurlitzer has taken away the darkness
Out there in the wild grass.
She has bought herself an artificial sun
To keep off robbers and rapists and everyone
Who covets what Mrs. Wurlitzer has.

Mrs. Wurlitzer has a voice like a public-address system.
Her arms fold with a snap! across her chest.
She trundles herself along the walk like a wheelbarrow;
No weed dares poke his head out in her lawn.

But she has not yet noticed that when the big light
Comes on at dusk, under the silent oaks
The shadows are blacker than ever. Anything
Might hide-and-seek there. I think the joke's
On Mrs. Wurlitzer.

TORNADO SEASON

Just as last winter's bastion
In your own backyard
Where pockets of last-ditch resistance
Are holed up in the spongy ground
Falls, before the assaults of March,
In the Central Office
Of the Disaster Preparedness System
A manicured bureaucratic finger
Pushes the button
That sends the children scurrying
Into the bowels of the school,
Where they are instructed to kneel
In the identical attitudes
Assumed by the Old Ones
In the face of Nature's quixotic demonstrations.

The sinister spiral
That comes whirling out of the west
Can pluck you naked
As a supermarket chicken.
It can snap civilization to kindling;
It is not swerved from its path,
It is not propitiated,
Even by the amplified u-lu-lu
Of the Disaster Preparedness System.

A DIFFERENT KIND OF RANDOMNESS

In the dream, the children are changed
Into two cats, one of which I recognize,
And a half-grown mongrel tied with a fraying rope.
We are all traveling together
In a rough cart, through unfamiliar streets
Under a dirty sky
When suddenly the rope snaps
And the dog runs off, limping a little.
I would run after him
With splints and bandages
But he is already lost under the feet of the crowd.
One kitten mews in the cart.
I remember your dream, how I butchered the cat
And fed it to you in a stew. I am alone
In a stone courtyard already dusted with snow
Of which no two flakes are ever exactly the same.

THE DAY THE HOUSES SANK

The day before the houses sank beneath the waves
there was an invasion of monarch butterflies
streets blazed in beating bronze
air shuddered like molten metal
trees turned to sunlight
roofs fluttered
pulsing above the chimneys, they made a cloud
everything darkened
Warning:
north central county under a yellow alert
until ten o'clock tonight
but the monarchs, passing, passing
were not stayed in their flight

Next day the houses sank beneath the waves
first the foundations, lapped by the oily tide
then lintel, windowframe, brick, eaves, tile, slate
now in the watery light wave after wave
rolls overhead, crests, passes, and subsides

THE DREAM-ADDICT

The boyhood friend
Wants to talk about *those days*.
He says in *those days*
They were beachcombers,
Buccaneers,
Firemen putting out the fires of the world.
Their single stride was a mile long,
Their sharp eyes missed no grass-blade,
He remembers how brave they were,
And how they tramped for hours
Carrying the gift of fire to the world.
When he thinks of *those days*
His eyes seem to glow,
His muscles contract
Like the legs of an old hunting-dog
Twitching in his sleep.

The boyhood friend believes in *those days*
Before time's mice
Nibbled his life to ragged lace;
Before bad-stepmother Time
Took him, father-by-accident,
And turned him into a dentist.

Now he is hooked on dreams,
A dream-addict.
His children's names
Are Memory, Hope, Illusion, and Disappointment.
His future has slid into the past
In the form of what once was the future.
He is come into his true and only season;
It is familiar to him
As the landscape of a bad dream.

THE BROTHER POEMS

The Dream

Her brother dreams himself
Small again
Curls like a girl's
Legs too short to run

Here in the dream
It is always Thanksgiving
Mother in the kitchen
Out of sight

Auntie kneads him
Into her bosom
Pinching and squeezing
She will stuff him with love

He is the Birthday Boy
They have put a knife in his hand
But he can't bring himself
To draw blood

With a single stroke
It would all be over
But his hand of a baby
In the dream, clutches nothing

The Secret

Her brother knows the password
To the deserted clubhouse of childhood
Even blindfolded he finds the way

Down that uncertain path
Hidden in the tall weeds
To the threshold of adventure

He has stood there before
Knocking to be admitted
To the society of heroes

Who have now disappeared
With the secret
Into silence and whispering dust

That Place

Her brother's friend
Victim of a cosmic mistake
Died someone else's death
Outside San Antonio
In a screaming of brakes
Wailing
Of the hot Texas wind.

She is still mourning him
Although he was not her friend,
A pale weedy boy
Driving a big car
A long time ago
Too fast and too far
To meet the wrong death
Along the bleak verges
Of the Lone Star State.

Earth has no memory.
In the roadside grass
Stiff and pale under the
Flat light of Texas
Nothing remembers.
If the wind wails
It is not for him.
Three times, she has passed
That place, without recognizing it.

Hide-and-Seek

Her brother is hiding from her
Inside this fat uncle:
Fingering his false moustache,
He pretends to be bald,
Trundles himself through crowds of businessmen,
Opening his mouth
To let out their father's laugh.

Once she and he had such an uncle;
When he came to visit
They'd run and hide.
Even after the scolding they weren't sorry.

She wonders if mother
Could flush her boy out of hiding,
The bold one, who set out each morning
To grasp the gold ring on the merry-go-round!
Now their father's signet
Hangs heavy on his ring finger,
And a sad man is telling her
His life is over.

She thinks inside there
Her brother is watching,
Waiting for the moment
When he will jump out
To say it has only been a joke,
He didn't really mean it.

THE STRANGER

This woman
With her marshmallow face
Extruded from a body made of marshmallow
Has come into the roadside grocery
In order to attack me

Alongside her pale flowered dress
Her hands hang, blunt instruments
She is hostile as a razor
Her veins pulse with poison
She pretends to be invisible

Having set and combed out her hair
She painted her lips
Eased her feet into those tight shoes
Counted out money for groceries
Preparing to destroy me

Clutching a loaf of cottony bread
And a dozen eggs
She is telling the cashier
The mere fact of my existence
Threatens her.

THE ASSASSINATION-KITCHEN

Epicure of conspiracies,
Night after night among wrecked coffee-cups,
Mutilated butts jettisoned in saucers,
He sifts through paper mountains of documents
Scrutinizing old recipes
For the secret ingredient that makes murder.

The assassination-kitchen swims in bleary light;
His table is littered
With crusts and crumbs of stale crimes:
Master-chef of corruption,
He prepares a sauce of nostalgia
For unappetizing old felonies.

Kettles hiss on the stove,
Skillets and saucepans sizzle—
A stench rises in the oven,
Something malodorous is boiling over—
He thinks he has found it!

Over a blue flame
Simmers an inedible stew
Of kidnapings, bombings, atrocities,
Terror in the kindergartens,
Spoliation of subway trains,
Respectable people fattening on blood-gravy.

MOURNING FOR UMBRELLAS

I have attended the funeral
Of the king of the umbrellas
Proud ruler of a dwindling race
At graveside I stood
In a little cluster of mourners
With high round shoulders
They had come from all over
Hastily summoned for this final rite
To do him honor for the last time
Where an umbrella walks
Is his nation
Citizen of no place
Owner of no property
He does not pay any taxes
His children do not go to school
He does not inhabit the cities but infests them
Like a plague of mice or cockroaches
He takes his own
Wherever he finds it, without asking
The suburban burghers hate him
They have driven him out
The downfall of the cities
Has had as one of its tiny by-products
The genocide of the race of umbrellas
The few who are left
Walk wearily, like very old men
Hunched in the rainy night

THE KITES

It is March. They are flying
kites from the library roof:
a red child with a green and yellow tail
and a blue child with a tail of yellow and red
pass swiftly by my window, sailing up
the air. Sail quickly past
my window, climbing the air.
                                They are flying!
Brothers and sisters, friends and cousins, bounding
up the windy steps of March, on the roof
of the sky. They are kites! They are
specks of confetti, tied
to other specks below on the library roof
which is flying too. Majestic and aloof
as earth itself, it wheels, dips, somersaults—
                                And we inside
windows are flying, too—
and birds, beasts, brothers,
friends, others, all
with trees, rocks, rivers and mountains,
railroad trains, automobiles, apartment houses
aloft! With satellites and astronauts
and the stars in their courses

THE HOUSE

When the house is ready I am ready
When the corners have swallowed
The last mouthful of dust
When the mattress turns over
In the sheet's embrace
When the bathroom tile gives me the wink
The house and I will take off together
On a flock of little wings
Into the stillness of two o'clock

The sky is speckled with twists of absorbent cotton
A child flies past furiously astride
A plastic dragon
The street stretches out before us
Doing nothing
The trees are watching out for us
A neighbor twitches the curtains of her eyes
Angrily into place
Pretending not to notice we are leaving

In time the house will settle down
Inside, I shall have arranged myself
I'll make myself comfortable
As a hermit crab in a shell
Now the adventure is over
The telephone number appears in a directory
Free offers addressed to no one fill the mailbox
The crippled and blind stand on the doorstep
And the neighbor sends to borrow a cup of flour

THREE

ARTIFICIAL ILLUMINATIONS

> "If, in physics, one seeks to explain the nature of light, no one expects that as a result there will be no light. But in the case of psychology, everybody believes that what it explains will be explained away."—Jung

First

Isn't that the way it happens to most women—one day some strange man walks in off the street and leaves her with a dirty house, a sink full of unwashed dishes, rooms full of unmade beds, and a mountain of soiled laundry? And there are likely as not a couple of loutish boys taller than she is, or a girl or two as well, with big, dirty feet and a loud, rude mouth.

He's gone, unrecognizable; and Baby's gone, too, all the babies have disappeared. Here there are only these overgrown barbarians, thumping on the tables demanding to be fed, with rips and rents in their clothing, savage songs on their lips—or lying lumpishly upstairs in frowsty beds.

In the neat suburban streets, nobody mentions the guerrilla warfare that is taking place inside every house on the block, where the giants are making themselves at home. No one wants to admit it is happening. No one wants to alarm the neighbors, whose houses, everyone knows, are immaculately kept, swept, dusted, polished, sanitary, and smelling of lemon.

Second

There was a girl—let's call her Maria—who all through her precarious adolescence thought she wanted to be a dancer. "For Chrissakes, stand still, Maria," her brother would yell at her as she cleared the table with a *pas de chat* and vanished into the kitchen.

"I can't stop, I can't stop dancing," Maria cried. She dressed in tights and leotards and tied her hair back with a ribbon.

She had no ear for music, but she sang all the time, la-la-la.

"Shut up, Maria," yelled her brother, putting his fingers in his ears and screwing up his face into an expression of pain.

"I can't, I can't," Maria cried as she danced out of reach.

Still dancing, she left home and went out into the wide world. The days piled up into weeks, which turned into months, and then,

49

although she didn't notice, into years. She thought if she had a husband, she could keep on the same way; why not?

In a judge's room she was married to—let's call him George—and they kept on exactly as before. "La-la-la," Maria sang; George thought it was charming. The baby was a darling, staggering around and laughing, dancing, and things were better than ever.

What happened? Where has George gone? Maria has suddenly shrunk, dwarfed, at bay; Baby has vanished.

Instead, there is a girl in the kitchen who sings so loud and off-key that all her brothers and sisters yell, "Shut up, it's awful, shut up," but she only laughs and cries out, "I can't, I can't," marking time until she can leave home and dance out into the wide world.

Third

Once there was a woman who gave birth to a dog. Her husband was very angry.

He said, "This is an outrage! For better, for worse—I agreed, but this is something I never bargained for."

The wife calmly lay back on her pillows. Next to her, cuddled in among the sheets, lay the dog. "Isn't he beautiful?" she murmured.

"He looks all wrong to me," said the husband. "He is uglier than any child I ever saw. He has bowlegs, and is covered with fur! His ears are too long! He even has a tail! I don't see how you can stand to have those eyes of his staring up at you."

"He is a perfect specimen," the wife said fondly. Nothing seemed to bother her. Of course, nothing bothered the dog-baby, which lay stupidly content in the mother's bed, its long, pink tongue, the color of boiled ham, lolling wetly out of its mouth. Now and then it would butt its blind, blunt nose against her breast as a sign that it wanted to nurse.

The husband gritted his teeth. He stamped on the floor and shook both fists in the air. He hated the dog. "This is too much!" he yelled, in a paroxysm of fury.

50

It was true that when the puppy nursed it was more repulsive than ever. In the ecstasy of its satisfaction it drooled out of both sides of its mouth, so that not only the mother's nightgown, but the sheets and blankets were soaked. Of course, it was not house-broken. When in a few months the dog grew old enough to run around, it left its disgusting messes all over the house. The husband never knew when he was going to put his foot into something really nasty. The dog was a sloppy eater, too, and the floor of the kitchen all around its dish was littered with dried-up or still viscous chunks of unrecognizable animal flesh that it had nosed out of its dish in its greedy haste.

"I can't stay in the same house with that monster," yelled the father. He slammed the door so the whole house shook. One day he tried to kick the dog, but he missed. Another time, he threw one of his heavy hiking boots at the animal. Not only did the dog get away, but as soon as the father sat down in his chair, burying his head in his arms in despair, the dog came running to him, wagging its tail, its eyes wet with love. As the poor man sat there, the dog threw itself on its back on the floor, presenting its furry belly to be scratched.

"Agggghhh!" screamed the man. He tore out great tufts of his beard and banged his head against the wall.

"Why are you carrying on like this?" inquired his wife. "I am afraid I'm unable to tolerate such behavior any longer." With that she put on her hat and walked out of the house, leaving the hus-band and the dog in there together.

Fourth

My sister thinks she is being punished for something, she doesn't remember what. Is it on this account she has brought forth twin girls? Every day she is forced to watch her own impulses, noble and ignoble, being acted out in terms so crudely literal, she can't help but be embarrassed and humiliated. If from the mouth of one

51

comes childish babble, the other, shameless, spews out the obsceni-
ties of the street. If the one scowls and snarls, the other cuddles
and purrs. Must she choose one to love?

The neighbors will understand if she chooses this one, saying it
is because she is sweet and pretty. But if she chooses the other,
they will credit her with all the virtues she doesn't possess.

This one she has named Amazing Grace, washed her, kissed and
taught her, held her confiding hand in her own. Some call her
Perfect Love.

The name of the other one is Eve; I have seen the four angels of
her face, the recurrent, the timeless, the present, and the forgotten.

My sister thinks she must have done something wrong, although
she can't remember what it was. Was it being born a woman in the
first place? In her flawed life she knows she is entitled to nothing.
Even nothing is second-best.

But watching the children at play she thinks her heart, which is
the size of a fist, is charged with more power than Union Electric.
If that energy could be harnessed, she thinks, it could light the
world.

Fifth

He wasn't right for a father. When they stood him up next to that
portly figure whose judgments reverberated, rumbling like thun-
der, from horizon to horizon, they all knew it. Or when he peered
around the partially opened frosted-glass door of the office at the
ungainly desk, its important papers, its heavily creaking chair, it
was clear he'd never sit there. Even less when at table he dished
out the main course, carving the fowl in his clumsy backhanded
way, giving everybody the wrong parts, a leg to the one who
wanted a wing, nothing but a neck full of bones for Grandma, who
preferred the white meat, and always forgetting the gravy—it was
clear that something was wrong. Even his clothes were wrong, he

didn't wear a vest or a hat, never polished his shoes, but slouched moodily in washed-out jeans they could hardly tell from the boys' when they pulled them out of the dryer.

They thought if it wasn't too late, maybe they could exchange him for something more practical. A new vacuum sweeper or cordless hand-held electric garden shears that they'd seen on television would certainly be useful; but at the last minute they realized that the dog could never learn to recognize an electrical appliance. So long as the dog wagged his tail whenever he came into the room, jumping up and fawning on his trousers, all but losing control of himself in his joy and peeing on the carpet, there was nothing to be done but keep him.

Sixth

First she gave away the things there was no room for. His desk, his books, his chair. Where could she put them in her three little rooms? Enough that she clung to the dining-room buffet, the enormous, crowded china closet, eight massive chairs, and the table, formerly the festive board, much too big for the tiny space.

Even her roasting pan was too big for the oven.

Into three closets were stuffed the mementoes of a lifetime. An overstuffed sofa; two oriental lamps with silk shades and jade finials; record player in a Chippendale cabinet; silver pitcher and tray, once wedding gifts; crocheted lace cloth made by herself with obstinate arthritic fingers.

Food from the kitchen cupboard she gave to the cleaning woman, jars and cans, boxes, too, leaving in the refrigerator with its burned-out bulb only some moldy cheese, and a head of lettuce, a few packages of frozen meat, and a can of coffee.

She gave the electric clock, the little radio, and her good fur coat to a neighbor in the building.

The elevator man got a vase from Italy.

At night when she couldn't sleep, she sat up, tearing old letters and diaries into pieces. Photos, too. All the old snapshots of the children. Into the incinerator they went.

Her cherished sewing machine she gave to a daughter-in-law who never used it and finally took it to a jumble sale at the school, where it fetched $18.

Nevertheless, they never suspected, until they had to pack a bag for her when she was put into the hospital, that she had given away everything. Her bureau drawers, that had held linen handkerchiefs, underclothes made to order by a Madison Avenue corsetière, crêpe-de-chine nighties, nylon stockings in padded satin cases, all were empty—or hid a tumbled mess of rags. Her shoes, in which she used to take so much pride, where were they? Dresses, coats? Nothing remained; a cacophony of wooden and wire hangers jangled lonesome in the closet.

Piece by piece she had divested herself of all those outer trappings of her woman's life, retreating within herself, becoming invisible, vanishing, shrinking into the shriveled kernel that was herself. Right under their very eyes she had done it, a sleight of hand that left them with nothing but what she would have most liked to be rid of, her heart, that obstinately clung and would not let go, insisting that they all keep time to its inexorable beat.

Seventh

They thought they had been summoned to a funeral, and came in their black clothes, with sad looks on their faces, expressive of grief; imagine their surprise when they found, instead, a marriage ceremony under way.

Hastily rearranging their expressions, they constructed a wedding bouquet out of the floral offering previously intended to decorate the grave. They wore their coats inside out, tied up their hair with colored ribbons, and poured champagne into their mourning slippers. The funeral baked meats were served up as the

54

nuptial feast; at high noon they breakfasted on rice and wedding cake. The groom toasted the bride, and the bride the groom; she wore lace, in summertime colors.

Under the sky a man of God presided. The sweet turf echoed to the feet of the bridal procession with a hollow sound. Climbing together into the new-made, skillfully carpentered box lined with rose petals, the newly married pair paused for one final salute as the spectators applauded under the empty blue arch of the sky.

The afternoon held its breath.

Far off, a choir began to sing a chorus of rousing affirmatives, thin and insistent as the dry, high song of the cicada.

Eighth

After the ball was over, they looked around and saw that they were still in the provinces. In spite of their strenuous exercise, they had come no closer to the centers of culture, the courts of love and beauty, than before. In fact, if anything, what they had wished for had receded even further into the distance; curiously, it seemed to have traveled from the future into the past without ever passing through the present, which was where they lived.

Taking off their hats and waving them in the air, they yelled, "Here we are, this way," but there was not even an echo.

Then they got into their separate cars to drive out along the avenues of the looted city to their suburban houses, full of the treasure trove they had appropriated.

Happening to glance back in that headlong flight, one of them thought he caught a glimpse of what they had all been seeking; but he knew it was impossible that it lay behind them, so he never mentioned it to anyone.

REINVENTING AMERICA

1. Reinventing America

In the house next door they are reinventing America. They draw abstract figures, rectangles, triangles, squares, circles, ovals connected by straight or curving lines. Here they sketch in Mother's sweet face, there Granddaddy's old frown, and even Baby, playing with her toes. They paint a factory, a lighthouse, a skyscraper, a silo, a church steeple. An ear of corn. An Indian. A bison. Mountains! Deserts! The nuclear disaster at Three-Mile Island! A high-school musical show. They fashion wax models of Mickey Mouse, Marilyn Monroe, and Rudolph, the Red-Nosed Reindeer. In fair italic script, they write *In God We Trust*. By the rude bridge that arch'd the flood they raise the flag of Iwo Jima, and fly to the moon.

But now it's suppertime! They tear off the paper they have been working on and crumple it into the wastebasket. Tomorrow they'll have to start all over again.

2. At the Hairdresser's

She glances into the mirror, half-expecting to see the promised transformation into a beautiful stranger. Instead, with an involuntary twinge of what can't, surely, be disappointment, but only the shock of recognition, she finds there only the same, all-too-familiar face. It's grown a trifle long in the jaw, perhaps, with the faintest suggestion of wattles under the chin; lips compressed, expecting the worst; eyes protected behind glass. Above, her own hair is tickled and teased into the shape of fantasy.

3. Shoes

Shoes make the best pets. They don't fawn, aren't hypocritical, self-centered, or greedy, and don't ever tell lies. They will go for a walk whenever you choose, or stay quietly in the dark closet without complaint. They don't get sick. Alone or in a crowd, they will stand by; they are not deterred by snow or bitter weather, and can withstand summer's heat as well. They don't bother the neighbors, and even the most restrictive condominium will admit them. They do not jump on you, leaving muddy prints, or shed all over the carpet, or scratch the furniture. They eat nothing, and drink not even as much as the most modest houseplant. A soft rub with a cloth now and then is all the attention they require. At home or abroad they are faithful companions, bearing no rancor even when kicked aside.

4. Divestiture

After years of adorning herself in the fashionable trappings of domesticity, his wife has peeled down. She has stripped away the garniture of kitchen counters; removed accoutrements of range and ovens; slipped out from embellishments of saucepan and skillet, casserole and tureen; left behind the ornaments of forks and ladles; flung away pots and kettles, plates, platters, basins, and bowls; rid herself of the frippery of the kitchen sink. Has she left herself not a cupboard to hide in? She'll be naked as Eve, with not a fig leaf remaining in the garbage can.

5. The Disappearance of the Hat

One of the best kept secrets of the postwar period has been the disappearance of hats. Where did they go? What has become of the hundred of thousands, no, thousands of thousands, or hundreds of thousands of thousands of bowlers, homburgs, toppers, fedoras and boaters that in former times crowned every manly dome? And the bevies of ladies' bonnets, sailors, cloches, berets, tams, toques, and pillboxes with their artificial roses and cherries, their ribbons, rosettes, and ruchings, their pleatings and plaitings, their flutings, their gauzy veils—in some enormous attic they lie dreaming, stuffed into musty boxes or strewn helter-skelter in vast heaps, awaiting the enchanted touch of a museum curator of the future.

57

6. The Mother

The role of the mother is always secondary. She plays, invariably, a minor part, peripheral to the central action of the drama. Perhaps she enters the drawing room through a door stage left, and crosses to the French window at the rear. Or, in an outdoor setting, clumps past, a dark-visaged hag, with a basket of laundry or kindling. In comedy, we applaud her flighty ways. In a proletarian piece she remains offstage, leaving the scorched beans and drying diapers to the young wife; and in classical drama—unless, a Clytemnestra or Medea, she turns on the very mother that she is —her pose is regal, sculptural, and calm: she is a monument, and not a woman.

Father William knew enough to be afraid of her when she learned how to use the knife in her hand, or when her shameless pulses drove the hot blood through her veins and her double-minded son brought down the throne of Denmark on her head and his.

7. Studying Western Civilization

In the Cabaret Voltaire, Mound City, Missouri, the pupils in the high school have made a model of the wheel, their latest invention. They are demonstrating it to an audience of cornfields, doctors, and hog-maw futures. Now they are inventing gunpowder, and the printing press. See what is printed: ETAOIN SHRDLU. Next, in quick succession, it'll be the incandescent bulb, the airplane, and the microwave oven. They are climbing Mount Everest, they are flying over the poles! Already they have discovered Goethe and Picasso, cloned Peggy Guggenheim, and are sending colonists to distant planets.

8. Visiting the Whales

Today the boats go out to visit the whales where they are resting offshore. How many are there? No one has counted them. Why do they linger here? Not all man's vaunted technology has succeeded in invading the Stygian deeps where they hold their invisible conclaves. Melville, setting out to hook Leviathan with his pen, was not more daring than we Sunday sailors in our cockleshell flotilla. Our spirits are high. Perhaps they will sing to us as we bob nearby in the gray Atlantic swells. Or perhaps they are waiting for us to serenade them; the sound of the flute and clarinet have been known to please pelagic ears.

With or without music, O great whales, sisters, you warm-blooded islands in the bitter sea, O mountains that breathe, that sleep, wake, give birth, die, and—yes, mourn—I would scatter a blessing on the waters for you, a blessing on the salt cold water that surrounds America, from which life springs.

FOUR

HOW TO MAKE A PRAIRIE

Big bluestem, little bluestem, Indian grass:
That's a start.
Then some native plants, red paintbrush,
Shooting star, blazing star, and giant compass,
Resistant to grazing, burning, and drought,
Appear among the grasses.
Here and there, sparse stands
Of prairie willow and blackberry; a few invading trees,
Red cedar, Osage orange, hawthorn and buckbrush,
Will find natural breaks in the sod,
Standing in shallow soil along outcrops of rock
Or in a drainage.
When the drought relaxes
In years of favorable rainfall, trees and shrubs
Will edge onto the prairie, and taller grasses
Creep from the drainages to higher ground;
But when the drought inevitably returns,
Trees are killed back to the old forest margin
Or devastated by wild fires, and the tall grass retreats
Once more into the draws, leaving a subtle landscape
Of open spaces, perspectives of sun-washed islands
Like isolated villages of natives threatened with extinction.
These are your prairie.
It will survive, through thirst,
Pitiless drying winds, repeated fires,
Or the trampling hooves of bison.
It will thrive.

THE ABSENCE OF A TRADITION

In the middle of our lives
We became emigrants
Without recognizing what was happening.

We thought it was a simple matter
Of moving from one house to another;
No frontiers to cross, no barriers
Of language or customs;

When we loaded the van
We said we were gypsies,
Traveling light, a moveable feast,
Free to choose going or staying.

Entering the new life
We settled easily into our furniture
Not noticing that we were in foreign territory;

But looking at what we have left behind
We are beginning to understand our exile,
And why the early settlers planted cottage gardens
With seeds from the old country.

REFLECTIONS ON HISTORY IN MISSOURI

This old house lodges no ghosts!
Those swaggering specters who found their way
Across the Atlantic
Were left behind
With their old European grudges
In the farmhouses of New England
And Pennsylvania
Like so much jettisoned baggage
Too heavy
To lug over the Piedmont.

The flatlands are inhospitable
To phantoms. Here
Shadows are sharp and arbitrary
Not mazy, obscure,
Cowering in corners
Behind scary old boots in a cupboard
Or muffled in empty coats, deserted
By long-dead cousins
(Who appear now and then
But only in photographs
Already rusting at the edges)—

Setting out in the creaking wagon
Tight-lipped, alert to move on,
The old settlers had no room
For illusions.
Their dangers were real.
Now in the spare square house
Their great-grandchildren
Tidy away the past
Until the polished surfaces
Reflect not apparitions, pinched,
Parched, craving, unsatisfied,
But only their own faces.

IN THE SUBURBS

In the suburbs I meet no one
No old man sunning himself
On an uncomfortable bench
Pretending to read the paper
No bored, underpaid office worker
Chewing a dry sandwich
No pasty-faced waitress in a tired uniform
No lovers stumbling to a rendezvous

Nobody's aunt devoured by fear of cancer
No bankrupt, no stockbroker, no owner
Of a small business
No factory worker in a blue shirt
No child and dog, partners in a dance
Careless in its choreography
No cat washing itself
No prowl car nosing along the curbstones

I too become invisible in the suburbs
I think I have made a landing
In the streets of an alien planet
Curving and recoiling to infinity
To the twittering accompaniment of a chorus
That repeats measure after measure without variation
Of a music virtually intolerable
To the human ear

A HOT NIGHT IN JULY

How slowly the leaves
Shuffle against one another
With a sound like paper being crushed
In a heavy fist
And the night presses down
Like dusty black felt
And the moon hangs there
Like an enormous paper lantern
With a single candle burning inside
That we once watched drifting higher
And higher over the terraced roofs
Before it burst into flames
And scattered ashes like flakes of dirty snow.

WALKING PAPERS

1

The light in her bedroom means
Somewhere two bodies are
Straining into one another
Stretched in the sweaty dark
Partly inside one another
Tonguing and fingering
While hidden in the black leaves
Of this heavy old tree
A stupid bird pours music into the air

2

Two of the streetlights are out
The darkness is thick
And soft as a velvet blindfold
Its blackness is stifling
It comes out of the ground
Escaping through woven grass
Wrung from the heavy dark leaves
A blind wind blows along the street

3

In someone's house
They're sitting up with a sick child
Croup, maybe, or one of those mysterious
Fevers the doctors can't account for
Tomorrow he'll prescribe something, but now
There's a long night to get through
Without dreams, unless sponging down
This child, dry and light as a cinder,
Is a dream

4

This street is asleep, or
Playing dead
All the eyelids of its windows are closed
No lights no voices
Even my footsteps are muffled
I have no shadow
I think I have been swallowed by the night
That here takes itself so seriously
Not even a firefly is permitted passage

5

A piece of the night detaches itself
It is my cat come to walk with me
He pretends he is alone
His tail switches from side to side
Disdainfully
In the globes of his eyes, that gleam
With a cold green fire
A gypsy could read the future

No shadow is disturbed
By the soundless prints of his paws

But deep in her dark house
Shuddering half-awake, lazily,
The earthquake-mother stirs

DÉJÀ VU

I have been here before
Laboriously climbing
The steep dull streets of this upstate town
Where the old Indian names are commemorated
In a huddle of brick the color of dried blood
Or on derelict signboards, platforms sinking to ruin
At the crossroads where the Indians believed
The soul might go astray

Searching in the dim public rooms
Of a decaying hotel
Among tables and chairs large and placid as horses
I have caught sight of myself in a mirror
Silent, monochrome
Moving through depthless space
With the fixed look of the blind
Unapproachable
As the princesses in the tall towers of history

I have wanted to abandon myself
To the weedy growth
Of hawkweed and plantain
Burdock and chicory
Shameless as a gypsy
Squatting on the margins of the world

SNOW

Upstairs they are shaking cold feathers
From thousands of pillows, again;
This is the same snow
That falls on my childhood
Out of the pages of the brothers Grimm
Over Fraülein's little house,
Carved all over like a cuckoo-clock;
The same snow, hardening at curbside
Into walls, towers, battlements;
Hanging white beards
On venerable buildings;
Snow solid as marble under a frozen sky.
And the same snow on Jungfraujoch,
When after a dinner of spiced red cabbage
We marched through the tourist tunnel
Into the glacier's glittering heart;
Snow on the roof of the world,
Snow from Alaska, Siberia, the poles,
Snow on New England, on the hills of Kentucky,
Snowplows airlifted to Cincinnati,
Snowdrifts in the streets of Memphis.
When the wind comes in, hugging the ground,
The snow rises and swirls in every direction
Like the snow in the glass globe of childhood.

BAKED POTATOES

I like to think of it all going on without me
As if it were a wind-up toy
Like my brother's mechanical train on its oval track,
An engine, a coal-car, two passenger cars, a caboose,
Going over the little bridge and through the tunnel,
Around and around when you wound it with the key,
To stop at the painted tin station. I like to think
That back there Dad is driving the Oldsmobile
Up the West Side Highway in rush hour.
The river is pewter
With facets of mother-of-pearl and highlights of salmon.
He squints through his glasses and grumbles at the traffic,
Impatient to be home with the evening *Sun*.
On Saturday Mother draws on gloves of glacé kid
Preparing for her assault on the department stores.
Riding home in the bus through the dusk she wonders
If Maggie remembered to put the potatoes to bake.
I imagine Maggie is dreaming, adrift at the window,
Leaning into the blue twilight, unaware
Of the surprises life is preparing for her;
I think of the baked potatoes, their coarse brown jackets,
Their steaming, mealy centers awash with butter
That Maggie will carry to the dinner table
As if back there it is all going on, without me.

PRAISE FOR WINTER

Because it is intransigent;
Because although there is no softness in it
It softens the harsh outlines of the world
Under its snow blanket;
Because you cannot make it love you;
Because the cold days are short, and at night
I can pull the house around me like a sweater,
And cat comes in to sit by the fire.

STOP-TIME

O poignant art of photography
O nostalgia of the camera
O patient, hooded eye of the lens
Awaiting the irrevocable *click*
Of the shutter, like a stiff eyelid
Closing on its final scene

O entrancement, O solace,
O endless ennui of the photograph album
On the parlor table of posterity
Weighted with the heaviness of the past
O dolor of the carousel of slides
Projected on the imperturbable screen

O ardor, O passion of seeing
O uncounted miracles of the visible world
And of the world invisible
O darkroom, chamber of the heart
Wherein all is revealed
As it will never be seen again

LIVING IN THE THIRD WORLD

Terrible things have happened in Jakarta
That you don't know about.
The man with a gun
Broke down their gate with his crowbar
And when the woman screamed
His shots went wild, and hit Dave.
Then Phyllis got sick.
They still don't know what it was, fevers and bleeding.

They say the air there is bad,
So wet and heavy, breathing it is a disease.
The little girls are homesick, and cry in bed
(The oldest got so bad they sent her back,
But she's out there now again).

In those extravagant jungles, even the blossoms
Exude a mephitic fragrance
And the people are different, smiling and sullen,
A villain in the shape of a young girl
Bringing strange, bitter foods without nourishment.

Where are the tea gardens, the nymphs
Who wove with graceful arms their innocent spells?
Are there no temple bells with sweet bronze tongues?

A beggar crouches in his own filth
Displaying stumps of fingers, running sores
He says the egg of the world is cracked
And from its wounds
Poisoned tears fall, like rain over Jakarta.

SAFE PLACES

The retreat to Vermont was orderly at first
Everybody expecting to find
At the end of the macadam, the old dirt road
Leading back into childhood
Expecting the luster of the farmhouse windows
As firelight burnished twilight
To make up for all they had lost
All they had left behind

So they marched like an army of refugees
Carrying lamps and birdcages, mattresses and clocks
Flowing along the highways of Vermont
Calmly as a river

But something went wrong

The simple hills that, from a plane
Look smooth and domesticated
Turned rough and wild,
Bears lurched through the wood
Travelers who wandered from the road
Lost all direction, starving or seeing ghosts

Even the road grew treacherous
As night fell, and neighbors
Eyed one another with suspicion
The safe places retreated from Vermont
Northward to Canada and the frozen void,
Or lay behind them, maybe, in the ruined cities

DRIVING TO MEXICO

Alongside the road
The mountains of the Sierra Madre
Are rising,
Heaving their bony shoulders up
Through the tangled desert.

One day they will throw off
The scratchy blanket of earth
And stand, on impossible legs.
Driving down to Mexico
I hear the thudding of an enormous heart.

ADVENTURES

Seventeen hundred miles from here
Under the arcades, an old man
Is setting out his yellowed photographs
Of a hero of the revolution
Whose life can be seen leaking out
Onto an exhausted mattress

What an adventure it is
Coming into one's life without knowing
What it will be like or where it will lead
Seeing in the mirror a face
One might not have chosen
Looking around at the other faces, wondering
Which are the heroes among them

The dead boy in the photograph
Had no time to imagine what it might have been like
To have escaped the bullets and become
An old man in the dim light under the arcades
Shuffling mementoes of adventures
Through a life he might not have chosen

THE FOREIGNER

The foreigner at the other table in the café
Tracing with a nervous finger the stain on the tablecloth
Asks if we know of a good doctor.
At home he is a respected personage,
A pillar of society.
Cast up on this shore,
With thin yellow fingers
He rubs at the tablecloth.
He asks what it is safe to eat,
If we are staying in the Hotel,
If the water is boiled.
Behind his left shoulder
The crack in the plaster is crawling slowly
Down the wall
And overhead
Incomprehensible laundry flaps on the line
With a sound like pistol-shots.
When the girl comes on noiseless feet
To refill his cup
His startled elbow jolts her arm
And he watches, appalled,
A fresh dark stain creep over the tired cloth.

LEAVING MEXICO ONE MORE TIME

Not the branch that taps at the window
Offering a single scarlet pomegranate
Not the grove of green feathers
Not the bird with wings of flame
Not the thin thread of smoke
Not the blue sky clotted with clouds
Not the lion-colored desert
Sleeping under a scratchy blanket
Not the 400-year-old walls
Crumbling at the side of the road
Not the huge sad trees
That stand in black pools of shadow
Not the acrid unmistakable coffee smell
Not the clatter of the great bells
Like tumbrils rolling over the cobbles
Not the heap of yellowing bones
With clumsy knobbed ends
Not the long twilights, needle-pricked
With sulfur-yellow patterns
Not images of Espagna
Nor the three tall cypresses
Bending and swaying toward one another
Like black-shawled gossips
Nor the old granny with eyes black as prunes
Nor the withered pod
Nor the dry seed of hunger
Not the simple broom of twigs
Scraping the stones
With a sound older than civilization
Leaving Mexico one more time
Precipitates a sensation
Heavy and cold as a stone
Because from now on
Something will always be missing

THE INVENTION OF ZERO

Without it, nothing exists.
Thinking of those ancient mathematicians
In their skin tents
Bending dark Semitic faces
In the odor of goat-turds and camel-dung
To decipher the hermetic universe,
Those venerable magi whose fastidious fingers
Dissected out this pearl
Of nothing, this naught, nil, nihil,
This iridescent bubble of wisdom, hollow at the core,
This insubstantiality, this absence,
This egg of being,
I am amazed anew
At the inexhaustible fertility of the natural world.

GRAPES

When you drive past the little stone bungalows,
Seeing the grapevines in Italian backyards,
Imagine a hillside in Tuscany
Drenched with sunlight the color of honey.

Imagine the young girls with bisque-pale faces,
Sure-footed as goats, skittering on stilt-heels
Past mysterious doorways
Up the steep cobbled streets;

And when you unwrap a bundle of sticks
Like dry brown bones, and press them
Into the unyielding earth of November,
Imagine the heavy clusters ripening under the leaves
Until you taste on your tongue the thin,
Aromatic bite of homemade wine.

MISSOURI

I'm none of you, Missouri,
With your old-time ebony or high-yaller blues,
Your sternwheeling, gambling, nothing-to-lose,
Your mustachioed, melodrama, flood-stage blues—
Nothing here I can use.

Nothing of you is mine.
None of your moonshining and banjo-strumming,
Your Bible belting-out hymn-shouting,
Your shotgun clay pigeon turkey-shoots,
Lewis and Clark, cottonwoods, barbecue ribs, your tall tales,
None of your Osage and Onondaga,
Your Irondales, Leadwoods, Mineral Points, Steelvilles;
I'm a stranger in Bonne Terre.

Where row crops on steep ground,
Robbing the soil, made gullies
Between the sinkholes and the ridges,
And old fields grew up in broomsage and blackberry,
Where your promised land
Turned sour under the plow, O pioneers,
I am a foreigner.

Don't want your crosscut saw, your halfmoon pies,
Your asafetida bag against disease,
Preaching all day and dinner on the ground,
Rag rugs, rail fences, chicken and dumplings,
Lamplighting time at dusky dark.
My beginnings are elsewhere, someplace
Dingy and dismal as an old ship's hold,
Or cramped in the bowels of a city
You couldn't begin to pronounce,
Far from your Red Top, Thorny Mountain, and Half Way.

After the spring floods, you show me
Aboriginal mud on the levee,
The river drowsing, torpid as a snake;
Show me your mound-builders,
How they lived, harmless as squirrels,
On acorns and wheat kernels;
Show me the red men,
The Frenchmen, Anglos, trappers and sharp traders,
The railroad- and brewery-builders;
Show me the toll-takers;
Show me the caves under downtown streets
Where runaway slaves used to hide.
Even inside, I'm an outsider.

Even after a hundred years
I'd be homeless on your homestead, Missouri,
A left-handed soul trapped in a right-handed body,
Homesick among the transplanted lilac and lily-of-the-valley,
Ill at ease amid your alien corn.
Unsettled among your settlers, never at home
In your Competition, your Braggadocio, your Charity,
My rootlessness is as American
As what made you, Missouri,
Chopping you out of the Ozark brush,
Breathing your life into the Mississippi mud,
Raising your rooftrees against the threatening skies.

AMERICAN SUITE

1

What binds me to America? These days
You have to fight it out at close quarters.
No more easy escape to the left bank,
Or the soft Mediterranean south,
Or the sidewalks of Barcelona;
Now it's every man for himself
On the home turf:
The man who feels like a rover
Trapped inside a householder;
A gypsy, trapped in the welfare state;
A brown-eyed man
Trapped in a blue-eyed body.
They say the scorpion will not bite
In the palm of your hand.

2

Where are you, America,
Making yourself thin,
Attenuating yourself,
Stretching yourself along the cutting edge
Of the frontier?

Are you out there
Lost in the tall grass?
Or wandering along the raw edges
Of cold and sleepy towns?

I think you are lying low,
Playing hide-and-seek
Between two oceans.

3

America envelops me;
Wherever I go
It wraps itself around me,
Hugs my shoulders,
A dusty pilgrim shawl.
My cloak of darkness,
My comforter,
I am swaddled
In its brilliant mantle;
Muffled and veiled,
I am concealed in America.

4

I'm a stranger here, America,
Like a summer visitor
Stepping delicately, barefoot,
On the hard sand
Between Moody and Wells,
Where the Atlantic's uncertain edging
Flutters like ragged lace
Over the dreaming shells,
And gulls grieve in rusty voices
Over forgotten losses;
Leaving footprints so faint
As to be nearly invisible,
And even these shadowy prints
Are wiped away by the tide.

5

With every breath
I breathe you in, America;
You are in my lungs, my blood.
Even my bones carry traces
Of your prodigal harvests,
Your weathers, your winds,
Your fluids, your ethers and vapors.
Even if I fly
Beyond our galaxy,
You go with me.
Inseparable,
We have become one another.

AT HOME IN AMERICA

These companions follow me everywhere
Crying out to be mistreated.
Her raddled face cries out,
Her mouth like a dry well,
Her eyes, red-rimmed, that open to darkness,
His lips, cringing away from a smile,
His hunched shoulders waiting for the blow,
Cry out. Their suffering
Announces itself, crude as a billboard,
Strident as an old-fashioned steam calliope.
But they do not want me to succor them.
They want me to turn on them,
To evict them, eject, expel, banish, discard them,
To say they are unclean
And contaminate the body politic;
That they are ugly,
And sully the beautiful image.
They say my refusal to turn them out
Punishes them, and so,
Unsatisfied, they follow me
Everywhere through America.

TO LIVE WITH A LANDSCAPE

1

Take your boulevards, your Locust Street,
Your Chestnut, Pine, your Olive,
Take your Forest Park and Shaw's Garden,
Your avenues that lead past street-corner violence,
Past your West End, past your Limit,
To shabby suburban crime,
Vandalism in the parking-lot,
Abductions from the shopping mall—
Like making the same mistake over and over
On the piano or typewriter keys,
Always hitting the wrong note—
How "very alive, very American"
They are, how chockful of metaphysics,
Hellbent to obliterate the wilderness.

2

Learn to live with sycamores,
Their sad, peeling trunks, scabbed all over
With shabby patches, their enormous leaves
In dingy shades of ochre and dun
Rattling like castanets, their roots
Thick as a man's leg, crawling
Like enormous worms out of the broken pavements,
Continually thrusting themselves up
From pools of shade they make,
Sculpturing the street
With dappled dark and light
As glaucoma, a disease of the eye,
Makes the world more beautiful
With its mysterious rainbows.

3

Already in Iowa the monarchs are emerging,
Signaling with their tawny wings;
In regalia of burnt orange and umber
The spangled imperial procession
Meanders along the democratic roadsides,
Across straight state lines,
Over rivers and artificial lakes
And the loneliness of middle America
On the way to Mexico.
The tiny wind of their passing
Is not even recorded
As a disturbance in the atmosphere.

4

Driving back into the American past,
Homesick for forests, flowers without names, vast savannahs,
Lowlands or mountains teeming with game,
Bluffs crowned with cottonwoods, mudbanks
Where crocodiles might sun themselves;
Finding instead the remains of strange picnics,
Replications of old selves, a cacophony of changes
Like a room crowded with chairs
In which no one can sit, as if history were furniture
Grown splintered and shabby;
Studying a picturesque rustic architecture
To master its splendid abstractions,
Shady verandas and porches,
Or the republican simplicity of a cow.

TAKING OUR DUE

We have always lived underground
In the woods, just below
The spongy surface of rotting leaves
Earth's steamy blanket

Or nesting under the flooring
In tumbledown barns
In the milky odor of animals

We find entrances
In wainscoting and baseboards
To unsuspected caves
Beneath the heavy-footed tramping
Of oxfords and brogans

Here we live as we have
Always lived
Demanding nothing
But taking our due
The crumbs that fall
From your unwitting table

PITT POETRY SERIES
Ed Ochester, General Editor